One Key Endless Freedom

Breaking Free with Christ

Keli Hargreaves

Copyright © 2022,2024 by Keli Hargreaves

All rights reserved. No part of this book may be reproduced, stored in a retrieval system, or transmitted in any form or by any means-- electronic, mechanical, digital, photocopy, or any other---without prior permission from the publisher and author, except as provided by the United States of America copyright law.

ISBN: 9798300220075
Imprint: Independently published

Unless otherwise indicated, all Scripture quotations are taken from the Holy Bible, New Living Translation, copyright © 1996, 2004, 2015 by Tyndale House Foundation. Used by permission of Tyndale House Publishers, Carol Stream, Illinois 60188. All rights reserved.

Scripture quotations marked (KJV) are taken from the KING JAMES VERSION, public domain.

Scripture quotations marked (ESV) are taken from the English Standard Version® (ESV®), copyright © 2001 by Crossway, a publishing ministry of Good News Publishers.

Scripture quotations marked (NKJV) are taken from the NEW KING JAMES VERSION®. Copyright© 1982 by Thomas Nelson, Inc. Used by permission. All rights reserved

Scripture quotations taken from the Amplified® Bible (AMPC),
Copyright © 1954, 1958, 1962, 1964, 1965, 1987 by The Lockman Foundation
Used by permission. lockman.org

"Repent." Merriam-Webster.com Dictionary, Merriam-Webster, https://www.merriam-webster.com/dictionary/repent. Accessed 20 Nov. 2024.

"Salvation." Merriam-Webster.com Dictionary, Merriam-Webster, https://www.merriam-webster.com/dictionary/salvation. Accessed 20 Nov. 2024.

"Renounce." Merriam-Webster.com Dictionary, Merriam-Webster, https://www.merriam-webster.com/dictionary/renounce. Accessed 20 Nov. 2024.

DEDICATIONS

I specifically dedicate this book to my mother Deborah Renee Bates, my father Thomas Wilbur Hargreaves, my sister Cassandra Stoner and most of all my children Christian Caldwell and Destiny Harrell.

It is also to all who have ever felt like an outsider, that they did not belong, were unloved, unwanted, or not shown the truth about Christ and his love for us. Last, but not least, any that still suffer in any kind of bondage or trauma. Freedom can be found when searching for Christ and strongholds of ALL kinds can be broken if willingness to let Him in and refurbish your broken heart.

1 *"The Spirit of the Lord God is upon Me, Because the Lord has anointed Me To preach good tidings to the poor; He has sent Me to heal the brokenhearted, To proclaim liberty to the*

captives, And the opening of the prison to those who are bound;
Isaiah 61:1 NKJV

18 "The Spirit of the Lord is upon Me, Because He has anointed Me To preach the gospel to the poor; He has sent Me to heal the brokenhearted, To proclaim liberty to the captives And recovery of sight to the blind, To set at liberty those who are oppressed;
Luke 4:18 NKJV

PREFACE

The spark of this book started in 2003 almost 20 years before it came to reality. It was my first tackle of recovery and Christ was always in my life. I didn't just do 12 step programs. I always knew my 'higher power' was and always would be Christ. Although understanding the depths of the spirit realm were still bleak.

I remember wanting to write a book about breaking free from addiction with Christ. The desire I now know was from God. The only issue was I didn't understand myself yet how to fully break free. As I ended right back later.

The missing link was the revelation to apply the Word of God along with my prayers and the understanding of breaking down mental strongholds and deliverance from so many things I was plagued by.

It began as only many studies from what the Lord had me apply to reach anyone needing encouragement over relief from loneliness, addiction and guidance in trials as I once faced. As it all started to unravel, God showed me an outline with all the many subjects that I had researched to get through some of my own battles, put together to serve as encouragement in many different areas of a life of somebody choosing to follow Christ.

As God was guiding me through the steps for myself to take to overcome my own battles, I had a strong desire to share with everyone that it might help. Help in their life to achieve the freedom and peace I received and even more strengthen their relationship with the Lord. As well as motivation to get in the Word. Here is the finished product.

Father God,
I ask to let everyone's hearts and minds be opened to what you want to be heard and understood, not what I think should be. This is written for your people to get something from you. I am only a tool. Please Lord, correct anything that is not from you, and bring peace and healing to all who read this.
In Jesus name Amen

MY STORY

With an introduction to Jesus at age 4 and in church till I was a teenager started me well but the things that plagued me from the beginning of life were still powerful and eventually overtook me.

A Runaway, pregnant at 16 then second child at 19. Chasing attention from guys and substances trying to cover depression and the strong Spirit of rejection. I quickly lost my kids which led me to find recovery to get them back. Managing to accumulate 3 years in one stretch and mostly 16 years free of hard drugs. Unhealthy men were still a big problem.

After many abusive relationships my kids moved in with their dads as I was losing my place at the time anyways. Soon homeless and recovering from surgery but still in pain and cut off medication I restarted the self-medicating actions of smoking meth and eventually trying heroin. Within a couple of months, I became an IV user for the first time, and it unleashed a side of me I never even thought possible. Many traumatic events, all forms of abusive situations 9 years of IV drug use, multiple hospital stays from suicide attempts to mental break downs to deadly infections and many trips to jail later.

I finally hit a point of surrender where even if my kids never wanted me in their life, I wanted to change my life for the better and return fully back to my savior that I was introduced to so long ago. Freed from generational curses too many to mention, soul ties that were created in a life full of promiscuity and abuse.

I am a completely new person. I am completely free from mental illnesses, healed from fibromyalgia and trauma, free from bitterness and rage, single and celibate over 2 years now and completely sober with no desire even when I have been in the atmosphere.

My heart will never leave those on the streets or battling addiction or mental illnesses as that is exactly where God pulled me from. I have been blessed with no desire to return even when exposed to the detailed environments of that life.

God wants me to use it to reach those others. Suffering as a prisoner in many forms for most of my life created a heart in me to expose the enemy, empower believers with their authority in Christ, and share the immeasurable power of God and freedom through Christ and the Holy Spirit. Every book written so far has been applications I applied to my own life with the Lord's direction that has continued to take me to new levels. Levels of intimacy and levels of freedom!

The Beatitudes

3 "Blessed are the poor in spirit, For theirs is the kingdom of heaven. 4 Blessed are those who mourn, For they shall be comforted. 5 Blessed are the meek, For they shall inherit the earth. 6 Blessed are those who hunger and thirst for righteousness, For they shall be filled. 7 Blessed are the merciful, For they shall obtain mercy. 8 Blessed are the pure in heart, For they shall see God. 9 Blessed are the peacemakers, For they shall be called sons of God. 10 Blessed are those who are persecuted for righteousness' sake, For theirs is the kingdom of heaven.
Matthew 5:3-10 NKJV

TABLE OF CONTENTS

Dedications	Pg 1
Preface	Pg 3
Introduction	Pg 13
What Is Salvation?	
Part One: Accept Christ	Pg 17
Part Two: Repent and be Baptized	Pg 23
Walking by FAITH	Pg 30
Breaking Free from Bondage	Pg 34
Beware of False Prophets	Pg 42
Generational Curses	Pg 55
The "Ties" That Bind	Pg 73
Be Transformed	Pg 83
Enlisted	Pg 94
Weapons for Freedom	Pg 104
Final Thoughts	Pg 114

12

INTRODUCTION

What if just believing is not enough? Has anyone thought of that? Or felt that after choosing to believe in Christ things only seem to get harder in your life. Truth is that John 15:18-20 states it will...

18 "If the world hates you, you know that it hated Me before it hated you. 19 If you were of the world, the world would love its own. Yet because you are not of the world, but I chose you out of the world, therefore the world hates you. 20 Remember the word that I said to you, 'A servant is not greater than his master.' If

they persecuted Me, they will also persecute you. If they kept My word, they will keep yours also.
John 15:18-20 NKJV

It also states that towards the end we will be hated and suffer great tribulation for Christ namesake.

9 Then they will deliver you up to tribulation and kill you, and you will be hated by all nations for My name's sake.
Matthew 24:9 NKJV

One thing that people forget is that though we may be persecuted for loving Christ, Christ repays us with the peace that only he can deliver inside us despite what the world hands us. Our full reward will not even be given to us here on earth.

12 Rejoice and be exceedingly glad, for great is your reward in heaven, for so they persecuted the prophets who were before you.
Matthew 5:12 NKJV

20 Then He lifted up His eyes toward His disciples, and said: "Blessed are you poor, For yours is the kingdom of God. 21 Blessed are you who hunger now, For you shall be filled. Blessed are you who weep now, For you shall laugh. 22 Blessed are you when men hate you, And when they exclude you, And revile you, and cast out your name as evil, For the Son of Man's sake. 23 Rejoice in that day and leap for joy! For indeed your reward is great in heaven, For in like manner their fathers did to the prophets.
Luke 6:20-23 NKJV

I am not only writing this to those that already know or follow Jesus and those that have a strong understanding around their faith. So, I will start around some basic things even some believers do not know or might not understand, as I didn't either and grew up in Church. Starting with the topic of Salvation. I want to flood your mind with the Word as you read so if you like to research, I encourage you to write verses down and cross reference them as we go. Ready, set, Go!

I pray you are touched by the Spirit and encounter Jesus in a deeper way from these words.
In Jesus Name Amen!

CHAPTER 1

What is Salvation? Part One: Accept Christ

Of course, most of us think of Salvation being when we ask Jesus to forgive us and come into our heart to save us, but do you know that the definition of "Jesus", is "God is salvation". And that Jesus is the only one by which we can be saved.

Yes, I am the gate. Those who come in through me will be saved. They will come and go freely and will find good pastures.
John 10:9 NLT

There is salvation in no one else! God has given no other name under heaven by which we must be saved."
Acts of the Apostles 4:12 NLT

8 But what does it say? "The word is near you, in your mouth and in your heart" (that is, the word of faith which we preach): 9 that if you confess with your mouth the Lord Jesus and believe in your heart that God has raised Him from the dead, you will be saved. 10 For with the heart one believes unto righteousness, and with the mouth confession is made unto salvation. 11 For the Scripture says, "Whoever believes on Him will not be put to shame."
Romans 10:8-11 NKJV

This shows us that just saying the words will not save us since God knows our hearts and knows if we truly have faith in him. We don't just want to repeat an empty prayer; we want Jesus to be our savior! So, if we really want salvation, we want to search our hearts to get the full benefit of becoming a follower of Jesus. We need to examine the conditions of our hearts before inviting him so that we do not end up like one in this following parable.

4 And when a great multitude had gathered, and they had come to Him from every city, He spoke by a parable: 5 "A sower went out to sow his seed. And as he sowed, some fell by the wayside; and it was trampled down, and the birds of the air devoured it. 6 Some fell on rock; and as soon as it sprang up, it withered away because it lacked moisture. 7 And some fell among thorns, and the thorns sprang up with it and choked it. 8 But others fell on good ground, sprang up, and yielded a crop a hundredfold." When He had said these things He cried, "He who has ears to hear, let him hear!" 9 Then His disciples asked Him, saying, "What does this parable mean?" 10 And He said, "To you it has been given to know the

mysteries of the kingdom of God, but to the rest it is given in parables, that 'Seeing they may not see, And hearing they may not understand.' 11 "Now the parable is this: The seed is the word of God. 12 Those by the wayside are the ones who hear; then the devil comes and takes away the word out of their hearts, lest they should believe and be saved. 13 But the ones on the rock are those who, when they hear, receive the word with joy; and these have no root, who believe for a while and in time of temptation fall away. 14 Now the ones that fell among thorns are those who, when they have heard, go out and are choked with cares, riches, and pleasures of life, and bring no fruit to maturity. 15 But the ones that fell on the good ground are those who, having heard the word with a noble and good heart, keep it and bear fruit with patience.
Luke 8:4-15 NKJV

Even if the soil in our hearts is not the best for growing faith, we can ask God to cultivate our hearts to receive the things that are available as children of God. Reading the Word of God especially out loud can change many things, but the condition of our hearts is an important one.

10 Create in me a clean heart, O God. Renew a loyal spirit within me. 11 Do not banish me from your presence, and don't take your Holy Spirit from me. 12 Restore to me the joy of your salvation, and make me willing to obey you.
Psalms 51:10-12 NLT

41 Watch and pray, lest you enter into temptation. The spirit indeed is willing, but the flesh is weak."
Matthew 26:41 NKJV

38 Watch and pray, lest you enter into temptation. The spirit indeed is willing, but the flesh is weak."
Mark 14:38 NKJV

If you have never asked Jesus to be your savior or want to recommit. I encourage you to pray this prayer...

Heavenly Father,
I know I am a sinner and have fallen short in my life and need a savior, I believe your son Jesus Christ came and died for my sins and rose again so that I would be forgiven and given eternal life. I turn my heart and life over to you now and ask that you show me how to live a life that pleases you and not myself or this world. Baptize me in your Holy Spirit and reveal yourself to me in my life. Thank you that I am now a child of God, Lord lead me along the path of everlasting life.
In Jesus name Amen

CHAPTER 2
What is Salvation?
Part Two: Repent and Be Baptized

Repenting is not just feeling remorse for things you have done but deciding to change your past choices that you are remorseful about and doing the opposite. To turn from it. This is the definition straight from Merriam-Webster.com

Repent
verb
re·pent ri-ˈpent
repented; repenting; repents

Synonyms of repent
intransitive verb
1 : to turn from sin and dedicate oneself to the amendment of one's life
2a : to feel regret or contrition
b : to change one's mind

6 "Therefore, tell the people of Israel, 'This is what the Sovereign LORD says: Repent and turn away from your idols, and stop all your detestable sins.
Ezekiel 14:6 NLT

4 John came baptizing in the wilderness and preaching a baptism of repentance for the remission of sins.
Mark 1:4 NKJV

3 And he went into all the region around the Jordan, preaching a baptism of repentance for the remission of sins,
Luke 3:3 NKJV

47 and that repentance and remission of sins should be preached in His name to all nations, beginning at Jerusalem.
Luke 24:47 NKJV

38 Then Peter said to them, "Repent, and let every one of you be baptized in the name of Jesus Christ for the remission of sins; and you shall receive the gift of the Holy Spirit.
Acts 2:38 NKJV

5 Jesus answered, "Most assuredly, I say to you, unless one is born of water and the Spirit, he cannot enter the kingdom of God. 6 That which is born of the flesh is flesh, and that which is born of the Spirit is spirit. 7 Do not marvel that I said to you, 'You must be born again.' 8 The wind blows where it wishes, and you hear the sound of it, but cannot tell where it comes from and where it goes. So is everyone who is born of the Spirit."
John 3:5-8 NKJV

Once we make our choice to repent and follow, we are told to be baptized. Publicly declaring we are choosing to follow our savior Jesus Christ.

16 He who believes and is baptized will be saved; but he who does not believe will be condemned. 17 And these signs will follow those who believe: In My name they will cast out demons; they will speak with new tongues; 18 they will take up serpents; and if they drink anything deadly, it will by no means hurt them; they will lay hands on the sick, and they will recover."
Mark 16:16-18 NKJV

If we look in a dictionary at the non-theological definition of salvation taken from Merriam-Webster.com. It states as a preservation or deliverance from danger or difficulty.

Salvation
noun
Synonyms of salvation
1 a : deliverance from the power and effects of sin
b : the agent or means that effects salvation
c Christian Science : the realization of the supremacy of infinite Mind over all bringing with it the destruction of the illusion of sin, sickness, and death
2 : liberation from ignorance or illusion
3 a : preservation from destruction or failure
b : deliverance from danger or difficulty

Which in my opinion explains more in depth of what can be accessed after asking Jesus by faith to forgive your sins and reside in your heart. Confessing and asking him to live in you is only the beginning. We can access far more than just freedom from hell and condemnation or even just peace in our hearts. Jesus gave us power over Satan in many other ways. Some of you may already know firsthand the power that is in the name of Jesus. Isn't it nice to hear that he not only saves us but can protect us from harm, and even bring prosperity to our lives?

16 For God so loved the world that He gave His only begotten Son, that whoever believes in Him should not perish but have everlasting life.
John 3:16 NKJV

If you didn't pray in the last chapter here is another chance if you changed your mind...

Heavenly Father,
I know I am a sinner and have fallen short in my life and need a savior, I believe your son Jesus Christ came and died for my sins and rose again so that I would be forgiven and given eternal life. I turn my heart and life over

to you now and ask that you show me how to live a life that pleases you and not myself or this world.

In Jesus name I pray, Amen

CHAPTER 3
Walking by Faith

7 For we walk by faith, not by sight.
2 Corinthians 5:7 NKJV

It can be a difficult thing to choose to trust in something you cannot see when so many things in life's experiences have shown that even things you can see have let your trust be violated.

1 Faith is the confidence that what we hope for will actually happen; it gives us assurance about things we cannot see.
Hebrews 11:1 NLT

17 So faith comes from hearing, that is, hearing the Good News about Christ.
Romans 10:17 NLT

By filling ourselves with the Word of God is how we can build our faith in the unseen. Then, when we see things, we read in the Word of God and it gets brought into our real lives it gives us more tangible evidence of His existence and furthermore increases that faith. Then the following scripture seems less impossible to our mortal minds.

20 "You don't have enough faith," Jesus told them. "I tell you the truth, if you had faith even as small as a mustard seed, you could say to this mountain, 'Move from here to there,' and it would move. Nothing would be impossible."
Matthew 17:20 NLT

Giving Christ control of our lives is the best decision we could ever make. Yet it takes the first step of faith to trust and journey into the unknown. If we are bankrupt emotionally or spiritually, we are at a loss for nothing if Jesus is not real. But He is beyond our wildest dreams, I promise. Do not take my word for it though, reach out to him and He will show you!

11 For I know the plans I have for you," says the LORD . "They are plans for good and not for disaster, to give you a future and a hope. Jeremiah 29:11 NLT

To access these plans and promises we need to be willing to change our lives and turn from evil. I had this problem in most of my life as I believed but did not always choose to get closer to God and learn of the things He was really calling me to. It can be hard work especially at first when all you've known is sin and bondage. If you were to give Jesus a trial run and give him everything you had to read his Word and do what he said for a month the things you would see in your life would not make you want to go back to your old life.

I pray you get encouragement and guidance from this and that the Holy Spirit fills you when you choose to take the step towards freedom and dedicate your life or even come back to him after being led astray.
In Jesus Name Amen

May God Bless the rest of your journey in Life by reading this!

CHAPTER 4

Breaking Free from Bondage

For some, admitting something like being a slave or under control of something other than ourselves can hit our pride. Being able to analyze our ability to have peace in our heads and turn from things that can be harmful is important if we ever want to truly feel and be free. Christ gave His life to free us from death and bondage. If we have been stuck in a lifestyle of sin, abuse, addiction, self-harm, depression, or sexual immorality we must dig for the deeper cause behind the actions in a spiritual and emotional way. There are spiritually unclean forces that can attach to us from past abuse or trauma. Also, things called soul ties and generational curses that if left unaddressed can even after being saved keep you bound to those destructive patterns. I will go into more detail on those subjects a bit later.

First, we will go into basic understanding about bondage and some scripture to fight against it. Bondage is slavery. Anything that holds us from who we want to be. It takes many forms; addictions are the most recognized. Isolation, sexual impurity, anxiety and depression qualify as well. Isolation and depression many times present itself before addictions take form. Many times, they stem from feeling like you do not fit in or lack self-confidence in yourself or your capabilities. Even just abandonment or rejection in your life. Realizing that the freedom that was sent long ago and continues, some of us do not see. Yet, it is in the Word of God.

3 Even so we, when we were children, were in bondage under the elements of the world. 4 But when the fullness of the time had come, God sent forth His Son, born of a woman, born under the law, 5 to redeem those who were under the law, that we might receive the adoption as sons. 6 And because you are sons, God has sent forth the Spirit of His Son into your hearts, crying out, "Abba, Father!" 7 Therefore you are no longer a slave but a son, and if a son, then an heir of God through Christ.
Galatians 4:3-7 NKJV

We were free from this long ago, but Satan will use lies to make us forget and slip back into it or keep us in the deception that freedom is not for us. That is a lie from the pit of hell. The Word states otherwise.

12 then beware, lest you forget the Lord who brought you out of the land of Egypt, from the house of bondage.
Deuteronomy 6:12 NKJV

6 'I am the Lord your God who brought you out of the land of Egypt, out of the house of bondage.
Deuteronomy 5:6 NKJV

15 For you did not receive the spirit of bondage again to fear, but you received the Spirit of adoption by whom we cry out, "Abba, Father."
Romans 8:15 NKJV

We do not need to settle for slavery to sin or any bondage. Jesus gave His life to free us from that and adopted us into heirs of His kingdom. How many people of royalty do you know live in a prison cell?

20 And Moses said to the people, "Do not fear; for God has come to test you, and that His fear may be before you, so that you may not sin." Exodus 20:2 NKJV

We are only called to fear God Himself no one else! This is not a fearful scared type of fear either. It is a reverent fear of knowing His power, the mercy and grace that flows through Him and choosing to honor that sovereignty by submitting. Submitting to the Lord can free you from the enslavement this world and sin bring.

The Word of God has authority over Satan and his lies. Stand against him and learn his tactics. He is slick and will use many things of this world to distract and discourage you from living in your identity in Christ. I urge you to study authority and identity in the Word of God. I have printable tools on this and many other subjects on the ministry website. My Strategies from Heaven workbook goes into a deeper understanding and application of identity if you want to go deeper. Once you ask Jesus in your heart you are instantly given the right to use the Word of God as a weapon. Knowing what to use and when are important tools in life.

7 Submit yourselves therefore to God. Resist the devil, and he will flee from you. 8 Draw nigh to God, and he will draw nigh to you. Cleanse your hands, ye sinners; and purify your hearts, ye double minded.
James 4:7-8 KJV

15 Speak these things, exhort, and rebuke with all authority. Let no one despise you.
Titus 2:15 NKJV

6 But the Egyptians mistreated us, afflicted us, and laid hard bondage on us. 7 Then we cried out to the Lord God of our fathers, and the

Lord heard our voice and looked on our affliction and our labor and our oppression. 8 So the Lord brought us out of Egypt with a mighty hand and with an outstretched arm, with great terror and with signs and wonders. 9 He has brought us to this place and has given us this land, "a land flowing with milk and honey";
Deuteronomy 26:6-9 NKJV

Let the Lord lead you out of your Egypt and into the land of milk and honey. He is waiting for you! This chapter is only an introduction to the freedom that is accessible. We will go into the basics of breaking off things not related to our own sin. Deeper deliverance is still needed many times. If you feel that is true for you. Look into finding it or contact me on website. We will set you up with either I or another deliverance minister to address your needs.

Father God,
Reveal the mighty power we have in Jesus' name to all who read this and guide them into a deeper understanding of the power that was given to us through Jesus. Who overcame the world and through Him, we can do the same.
In Jesus name, Amen

33 I have told you all this so that you may have peace in me. Here on earth you will have many trials and sorrows. But take heart, because I have overcome the world."
John 16:33 NLT

CHAPTER 5
Beware of False Prophets

I want to touch on a very important and under taught subject of "False Prophets." What they are, how many more of them there are than we think and how to test them and protect yourselves. I will start with the warnings straight from the Word of God. It is not to bring on paranoia but to recall the necessity of being aware "at all times." As a practice I encourage you to grab your bible and reference every scripture I share here to verify that I am in fact not delivering false information or even if it were to be a misprint that could lead you along with distorted information. Check things do not just trust because I say I am a believer that I am sharing sound doctrine. Test me and others. More than anything, get to know the Word and you will be quick to know if something contradicts it. If it goes against the Word be quick to reject it, no matter how popular the preacher is or how good it sounds.

1 Beloved, do not believe every spirit, but test the spirits to see whether they are from God, for many false prophets have gone out into the world. 2 By this you know the Spirit of God: every spirit that confesses that Jesus Christ has come in the flesh is from God, 3 and every spirit that does not confess Jesus is not from God. This is the spirit of the antichrist, which you heard was coming and now is in the world already.
1 John 4:1-3 ESV

1 I charge you in the presence of God and of Christ Jesus, who is to judge the living and the dead, and by his appearing and his kingdom: 2 preach the word; be ready in season and out of season; reprove, rebuke, and exhort, with complete patience and teaching. 3 For the time is coming when people will not endure sound teaching, but having itching ears they will accumulate for themselves teachers to suit their own passions, 4 and will turn away from listening to the truth and wander off into myths. 5 As for you, always be sober-minded, endure suffering, do the work of an evangelist, fulfill your ministry.
2 Timothy 4:1-5 ESV

7 For an overseer, as God's steward, must be above reproach. He must not be arrogant or quick-tempered or a drunkard or violent or greedy for gain, 8 but hospitable, a lover of good, self-controlled, upright, holy, and disciplined. 9 He must hold firm to the trustworthy word as taught, so that he may be

able to give instruction in sound doctrine and also to rebuke those who contradict it. 10 For there are many who are insubordinate, empty talkers and deceivers, especially those of the circumcision party. 11 They must be silenced, since they are upsetting whole families by teaching for shameful gain what they ought not to teach.
Titus 1:7-11 ESV

This is talking about our leaders and who we appoint and how deceivers are going to be coming especially from the circumcised, now this isn't just referring to the Jews but the people that have the strong tendency towards religiosity and ceremonial type ritualistic practices that were done away with at the cross. We no longer need a mediator like a priest or pastor to access our father. Jesus is that for us.

For, There is one God and one Mediator who can reconcile God and humanity—the man Christ Jesus.

1 Timothy 2:5 NLT

Yes, we need guidance into further discipleship and understanding of the Word but test EVERYTHING you hear from anyone leading you and ask the Lord for increased discernment of spirits so that you yourself will not be deceived.

1 Now the Spirit expressly says that in later times some will depart from the faith by devoting themselves to deceitful spirits and teachings of demons, 2 through the insincerity of liars whose consciences are seared, 3 who forbid marriage and require abstinence from foods that God created to be received with thanksgiving by those who believe and know the truth. 4 For everything created by God is good, and nothing is to be rejected if it is

received with thanksgiving, 5 for it is made holy by the word of God and prayer.
1 Timothy 4:1-5 ESV

Even the elect is at risk of being deceived so learn to test the spirits so that the deceived will not deceive you!

3 If anyone teaches a different doctrine and does not agree with the sound words of our Lord Jesus Christ and the teaching that accords with godliness, 4 he is puffed up with conceit and understands nothing. He has an unhealthy craving for controversy and for quarrels about words, which produce envy, dissension, slander, evil suspicions, 5 and constant friction among people who are depraved in mind and deprived of the truth, imagining that godliness is a means of gain.
1 Timothy 6:3-5 ESV

11 And many false prophets will arise and lead many astray. 12 And because lawlessness will

be increased, the love of many will grow cold. 13 But the one who endures to the end will be saved.
Matthew 24:11-13 ESV

24 For false christs and false prophets will arise and perform great signs and wonders, so as to lead astray, if possible, even the elect. 25 See, I have told you beforehand.
Matthew 24:24-25 ESV

    One thing some teachers teach is that we will only be facing false Christ's or Antichrist's which are known to be against Christ's teaching. Yet it says in the Word many times there will be many false prophets that will lead "Many" astray, even the elect. No one is exempt so always be on guard. More than anything, live a holy life and keep doors shut to sin. Yes, we are human and by nature sinners but if you are filling yourself with the Spirit you will be empowered to live that holy life. We cannot achieve this without the Spirit. So, seek the infilling and intimate time with the Holy Spirit. To walk as such.

22 For false christs and false prophets will arise and perform signs and wonders, to lead astray, if possible, the elect. 23 But be on guard; I have told you all things beforehand. Mark 13:22-13 ESV

Something we must look out for are those things that sound good, or we would like to believe, yet don't have biblical backup. If it says we will seek those teachers that fill us up with those things that sound good to suit our passions, then let's choose not to be the ones to seek out those false prophets and encourage them to continue to deceive us.

3 For the time is coming when people will not endure sound teaching, but having itching ears they will accumulate for themselves

teachers to suit their own passions, 4 and will turn away from listening to the truth and wander off into myths.
2 Timothy 4:3-4 ESV

15 It's true that some are preaching out of jealousy and rivalry. But others preach about Christ with pure motives. 16 They preach because they love me, for they know I have been appointed to defend the Good News. 17 Those others do not have pure motives as they preach about Christ. They preach with selfish ambition, not sincerely, intending to make my chains more painful to me. 18 But that doesn't matter. Whether their motives are false or genuine, the message about Christ is being preached either way, so I rejoice. And I will continue to rejoice.
Philippians 1:15-18 NLT

    I want to stress that you will not hear me speak out against a pastor or preacher as a false prophet and neither should you. I know we might think we are doing a service, however we are taking away from our own assignments and only feeding the spirit of division and sometimes just gets us stuck in criticism only opening doors to our own downfall. Let us not join them. Focus on our own refining and assignment. You can pray and leave it to God. He will handle those misleading His sheep and let us keep track of ourselves. If this is in your own leadership the Lord will lead you in that if you are to do anything but do not seek to find false things. That is a motive of the enemy to divide. Use discernment.

9 And if the prophet is deceived and speaks a word, I, the LORD, have deceived that prophet, and I will stretch out my hand against him and will destroy him from the midst of my people Israel. 10 And they shall bear their punishment--the punishment of the prophet and the punishment of the inquirer shall be alike-- 11 that the house of

Israel may no more go astray from me, nor defile themselves anymore with all their transgressions, but that they may be my people and I may be their God, declares the Lord GOD."
Ezekiel 14:9-11 ESV

Keep the hunger for seeking the knowledge of God, the Word and what the Holy Spirit directs you to yet always be aware of possible deception. Every morning, remember to put on your protection and lead your heart in the way of the Lord. Don't follow your heart like the World says but lead and guard it.

11 Put on the whole armor of God, that you may be able to stand against the schemes of the devil. 12 For we do not wrestle against flesh and blood, but against the rulers, against the authorities, against the cosmic powers over this present darkness, against the spiritual forces of evil in the heavenly places.

Ephesians 6:11-12 ESV

19 Hear, my son, and be wise, and direct your heart in the way.
Proverbs 23:19 ESV

Guard your heart above all else, for it determines the course of your life.
Proverbs 4:23 NLT

Dear Father,

I ask that the Word you gave me for these people will reside in their hearts and open up the vision and ability to know how to test spirits and knowledge that comes to them and give them confidence that they are obeying your Words and instructions not just ideas from false prophets. Let it edify each one to become more like you and be the best student of your ways so they too can be teachers of the same things they learned and build more disciples for your kingdom.

In Jesus Name Amen

CHAPTER 6
Generational Curses

We can investigate the sources for trials that seem to plague us and many times it can be linked to your bloodline. We all know the history of medical research in the findings of hereditary diseases such as diabetes, cancers, and even the commonality with addictions such as alcoholism or drugs that can run in families.

What if I was to tell you that you have more power in breaking that than just eating better from the start so that you don't get diabetes, having healthy habits in life to prevent the likelihood of cancers, or not taking a first drink or drug so that you don't end up with compulsive habits like past family members. These can possibly be rooted from curses in your family bloodline.

Some things that can be added as generational roots can be a repetitive occurrence of divorces, adultery, perversions, lust issues, premature deaths, child abuse, homosexuality, sexual abuse and even witchcraft that has been practiced in your bloodline and so many other things from past generations. Yet even if we are to not ourselves participate even when temptation arises it can eventually affect our children and their children if we don't break those curses. I will start with the first example of curses in the Bible with the story of Adam and Eve. Adam and Eve sinned. Afterwards, God cursed the serpent for his deception to crawl on the ground. He cursed the ground from bearing crops, and women with extreme pain in childbirth.

13 And the Lord God said to the woman, "What is this you have done?" The woman said, "The serpent deceived me, and I ate." 14 So the Lord God said to the serpent: "Because you have done this, You are cursed more than all cattle, And more than every beast of the field; On your belly you shall go, And you shall eat dust All the days of your life. 15 And I will put enmity Between you and the woman, And between your seed and her seed; He shall bruise your head, And you shall bruise His heel." 16 To the woman He said: "I will greatly multiply your sorrow and your conception; In pain you shall bring forth children; Your desire shall be for your husband, And he shall rule over you." 17 Then to Adam He said, "Because you have heeded the voice of your wife, and have eaten from the tree of which I

commanded you, saying, 'You shall not eat of it': "Cursed is the ground for your sake; In toil you shall eat of it All the days of your life. 18 Both thorns and thistles it shall bring forth for you, And you shall eat the herb of the field. 19 In the sweat of your face you shall eat bread Till you return to the ground, For out of it you were taken; For dust you are, And to dust you shall return."
Genesis 3:13-19 NKJV

Then we have their son Cain who is cursed for killing his brother.

8 Now Cain talked with Abel his brother; and it came to pass, when they were in the field, that Cain rose up against Abel his brother and killed him. 9 Then the Lord said to Cain, "Where is Abel your brother?" He said, "I do not know. Am I my brother's keeper?" 10 And He said, "What have you done? The voice of your brother's blood cries out to Me from the ground. 11 So now you are cursed from the

earth, which has opened its mouth to receive your brother's blood from your hand. 12 When you till the ground, it shall no longer yield its strength to you. A fugitive and a vagabond you shall be on the earth."
Genesis 4:8-12 NKJV

We also have the example that both generational curses and generation blessings exist by the fact that Adam and Eve sinning created all to be punished and with Christ's death brought the ability of redemption of salvation by believing in him and repenting. Now salvation frees us from death, but we can still be very affected by curses while we still live if we are unaware at the time of salvation to our full benefits list. In Revelation it talks about when Jesus returns there will be no more curse but not till then.

3 And there shall be no more curse, but the throne of God and of the Lamb shall be in it,

and His servants shall serve Him. 4 They shall see His face, and His name shall be on their foreheads. 5 There shall be no night there: They need no lamp nor light of the sun, for the Lord God gives them light. And they shall reign forever and ever. 6 Then he said to me, "These words are faithful and true." And the Lord God of the holy prophets sent His angel to show His servants the things which must shortly take place. 7 "Behold, I am coming quickly! Blessed is he who keeps the words of the prophecy of this book."
Revelation 22:3-7 NKJV

We do have the power to renounce and repent of our sins and the sins of our ancestors, and we are called to do so. We already visited the definition of repent. Now let us look at what Renounce means. Renounce on merriam-webster.com was defined as this:

Renounce

verb
1 : to give up, refuse, or resign usually by formal declaration
2 : to refuse to follow, obey, or recognize any further : repudiate

So when we renounce it like removing the inheritance of wickedness or sickness. And putting into effect the true inheritance given at the cross through Christ.

38 You shall perish among the nations, and the land of your enemies shall eat you up. 39 And those of you who are left shall waste away in their iniquity in your enemies' lands; also in their fathers' iniquities, which are with them, they shall waste away. 40 'But if they confess their iniquity and the iniquity of their fathers, with their unfaithfulness in which they were unfaithful to Me, and that they also have walked contrary to Me, 41 and that I also have walked contrary to them and have brought them into the land of their enemies; if

their uncircumcised hearts are humbled, and they accept their guilt--
Leviticus 26:38-41 NKJV

When we understand that we can walk in more freedom today as we breathe, it opens doors to have not only more peace in our lives but to allow God to use us in ways we never fathomed. Many of us are unaware of this power we have and how simple it is.

I was a believer at age 4 and grew up in Church. I suffered from serious depression and self-rejection most of my life even in elementary school. Then addictions, abusive and broken relationships, and even chronic mental and physical issues as I got older. Since being educated on this power I have, I have not needed to see my doctor for at least over a year even with this pandemic, I had serious chronic pain from many injuries and fibromyalgia and now barely need even Tylenol for anything. Diagnosed with bi-polar, panic disorder, ptsd, hospitalized multiple times for suicide attempts and mental breaks. Now not a trace of mental issues or even medicine for them for multiple years.

Free from being not only an active IV user of meth and heroin but being around it due to my ministry God called me to and not even wanting it. I never imagined that was possible. It wasn't at the beginning of stopping using drugs, but after I repented and renounced the specific curses that the Spirit had revealed to me that were in my life, EVERYTHING changed. This subject is one of the biggest motivators for me writing this book. I want to expose the power and freedom we truly have as heirs of Christ. Just as we have generational curses, we have generational blessings we can pass on.

1 Praise the Lord! Blessed is the man who fears the Lord, Who delights greatly in His

commandments. 2 His descendants will be mighty on earth; The generation of the upright will be blessed. 3 Wealth and riches will be in his house, And his righteousness endures forever.
Psalms 112:1-3 NKJV

More scripture on generational curses

9 I call heaven and earth as witnesses today against you, that I have set before you life and death, blessing and cursing; therefore choose life, that both you and your descendants may live;
Deuteronomy 30:19 NKJV

keeping mercy for thousands, forgiving iniquity and transgression and sin, by no means clearing the guilty, visiting the iniquity of the fathers upon the children and the children's children to the third and the fourth generation."
Exodus 34:7 NKJV

5 you shall not bow down to them nor serve them. For I, the Lord your God, am a jealous God, visiting the iniquity of the fathers on the children to the third and fourth generations of those who hate Me,
Exodus 20:5 NKJV

Freedom is at hand though; the key is in you and in the Word. Turn to it and achieve endless freedom.

31 Then Jesus said to those Jews who believed Him, "If you abide in My word, you are My disciples indeed. 32 And you shall know the truth, and the truth shall make you free." 33 They answered Him, "We are Abraham's descendants, and have never been in bondage to anyone. How can you say, 'You will be made free'?" 34 Jesus answered them, "Most assuredly, I say to you, whoever commits sin is a slave of sin. 35 And a slave does not abide in the house forever, but a son abides forever. 36

Therefore if the Son makes you free, you shall be free indeed.
John 8:31-36 NKJV

Breaking off Generational Curses

I encourage you to rid your life of the curses that the spirit reveals to you or that you see blatantly in your family and leave your generations to come with blessings instead. I want to see you all free and more than that Jesus wants you free! It is possible with the blood of Jesus Christ that was so graciously shed. Here are sample prayers to break some of these things off your life. Don't just read them though, say them out loud and apply them and get free!

In fact, grab a sheet of paper now and write down the ones you know. Then pray now if you have the ability to be free from distraction. Free from kids, phones, television and even spouses unless you are doing these prayers together. Music if it is worship is ok. Not that you can't do it with them. We want to pray that the holy spirit reveals to you any hidden generation sin that needs to be broken off now. Protecting from distractions helps to ensure hearing is clear and correct.

Let's pray.

Father God,
We come before you in search of any hidden generational sin, curses, sickness or generational witchcraft in our bloodline. Reveal them all now.
In Jesus name Amen

Next will be a prayer to cancel them and begin in a future towards freedom. Again, within an atmosphere free from distractions.

Generational Curses

I repent and renounce my sins and the sins of my ancestors and break these spirit(s) off my bloodline now. I release complete forgiveness to my ancestors for passing them to me. I break off the spirit of...........(read list and/or the following) Spirit of fear, idolatry, immorality, lust, all witchcraft or practices of the occult, perversion, abuse, addiction, bitterness, infirmity, perversion, abuse, depression, rejection and self-rejection, suicide, abandonment, pride, rebellion, poverty, unworthiness and inferiority, and any other spirits still unknown.
In Jesus name Amen

I receive my adoption into righteousness.
I loose acceptance, purity, faithfulness, love, obedience, confidence, provision, safety, power, love and a sound mind into my life.
In Jesus name Amen

Thank you, Jesus, for my freedom purchased on the cross. I praise you! Show me how to better serve you and grow in your liking.
In Jesus name Amen

If you know or believe your family practiced witchcraft or yourself did, such as freemasonry, Santería, rituals, tarot cards, necromancy, runes, divination, psychic powers, Celtic witchcraft, astrology, wicca, satanism, energy manipulation, reiki, yoga, martial arts, use of crystals, shamanism, native American religions, new age etc. If you are unsure, ask the Lord if it needs to be included. Pray the following as well as remove items connected to any of these from your home. Don't give them away either burn or destroy them if possible or in trash. As well there will be prayer to cleanse and bless your home after this.

Generational Witchcraft

Father God,
I now repent and renounce any of these sins of witchcraft known or unknown practiced by myself or my bloodline. I rebuke and bind every one of them. I detach myself and my family from all evil curses, fetishes, charms, vexes, hexes, spells, blood spells, blood covenants, every jinx, all psychic powers or prayers, sorcery, bewitchments, enchantments, witchcraft, love potions or demonic dedications that have been placed upon me or my family.
In Jesus name Amen

I detach myself from any monitoring spirits or familiar spirits assigned to me and let the Lord demolish every evil altar raised for my torment or destruction with His mighty right hand.
In Jesus name Amen

Prayers to cleanse and bless your home.

Take some anointing oil. Anoint every door and window. As you pray...

Father cleanse this house of all unclean spirits or objects, revealing anything that needs to be removed. I dedicate this house to you Lord. As for me and my house, we will serve the Lord. Anything not of God must leave now in Jesus name. I welcome your holy spirit to reside in myself and my home. Fill this place.
In Jesus name Amen

Father God,
I ask the Spirit to reveal to each one who reads this the power you have given them to walk in freedom and open their hearts to receive revelation in the areas that they can and need to break off. Send healing upon their lives as they begin to become who you called them to be. Free from the chains of our past bondages. And empowered by your holy spirit.
In Jesus Name Amen

CHAPTER 7
The "Ties" That Bind

We've all heard people talk about intimate partners, and how sleeping with someone is like you're sleeping with all the people they slept with. With most of the world's perspective this comes from a physical standpoint and explanation. What if I told you that there is also a spiritual aspect that is far more dangerous than just getting an STD or pregnant. One that in reality, contaminates your very soul. As it says....
When we sleep with someone, we create what is called a soul tie.

24 Therefore a man shall leave his father and mother and be joined to his wife, and they shall become one flesh.
Genesis 2:24 NKJV

And then again...

5 and said, 'For this reason a man shall leave his father and mother and be joined to his wife, and the two shall become one flesh'? 6 So then, they are no longer two but one flesh. Therefore what God has joined together, let not man separate."
Matthew 19:5-6 NKJV

There are Godly soul ties as well and they are not always only with those we are intimate with physically but there are ones with close friends and family that can be good ties. They are like a covenant relationship between one and another.

1 Now when he had finished speaking to Saul, the soul of Jonathan was knit to the soul of David, and Jonathan loved him as his own soul. 2 Saul took him that day, and would not let him go home to his father's house anymore. 3 Then Jonathan and David made a covenant, because he loved him as his own soul. 4 And Jonathan took off the robe that was on him and gave it to David, with his armor, even to his sword and his bow and his belt.

I Samuel 18:1-4 NKJV

This was an example of deep brotherly love without connection through blood.
Let me remind you that a soul consists of the mind, will and emotions. So, if you think about it, a soul tie will join those parts of you with that of another. Since we can't see other's emotions, thoughts or know what truly drives them, we need to protect ourselves from allowing an attachment like that to occur with someone still engaging

with demons we may not know they entertain or are tormented by. Therefore, we are not just strongly encouraged to not engage with sex outside of marriage. We are told to run from it.

18Run from sexual sin! No other sin so clearly affects the body as this one does. For sexual immorality is a sin against your own body.
1 Corinthians 6:18 NLT

It warns us about not becoming one with a prostitute showing we still become one even if we have sexual relations without marriage.

15 Don't you realize that your bodies are actually parts of Christ? Should a man take his body, which is part of Christ, and join it to a prostitute? Never! 16 And don't you realize that if a man joins himself to a prostitute, he becomes one body with her? For the Scriptures say, "The two are united into one."

I Corinthians 6:15-16 NLT

A good way to know if a deep relationship could be Godly or ungodly in foundation is to ask these 3 questions.
1. Do they encourage your drive to follow Christ or pull you away?
2. Do they bring out godly or ungodly behaviors?
3. Do you have healthy boundaries with each other, open communication, and trust or obsessiveness, miscommunication and bitterness towards each other at times?

What do we do when we have built these ties before following Christ or were given this understanding? We pray to break them and learn to keep yourself safe by walking by the Spirit from here on out. Signs you might have an ungodly soul tie that needs to be broken; you have been a victim of sexual abuse, emotional or physical abuse especially from family members. Another sign is, if you think of an ex or a song that reminds you of them and anger or extreme sadness come over you or even inability to function at a normal level even after years of breaking up, obsessive thoughts even after a long time after breaking up, things that used to trigger them start triggering you, when it never did before. Even if you don't see the effects, I went down the list and broke them with everyone I had a past history with and even unhealthy relationships with family members and friends that had triggered emotional issues in me. Ask the Spirit to reveal any ungodly ties that need to be broken. He will honor your desire to be free.

Note: Some soul ties have been created in situations of abuse. In that case the prayer will be different. With first being willing to release full forgiveness for the act. To disconnect trauma and/or bitterness that could have also entered at this time as well as the soul tie.

Prayer to break soul ties.

Heavenly Father,
Thank you for saving me from destruction. I praise you for sending Jesus to die for my sins. Specifically, I confess that I have sinned and created ungodly soul ties through practicing sexual immorality. I repent and renounce these acts. Wash me clean and bring to mind everyone I need to acknowledge consciously breaking these off. Return any part of their soul back to them and return any part of mine back to myself. I plead the blood of Jesus over any soul wounds that were created within this soul tie.

Restore my soul to how it was before. I renounce the act of sexual immorality and ask for your spirit to give me the discernment and strength to walk in purity and keep my temple holy. In Jesus name.

Restore me to wholeness in spirit, soul and body and reintegrate any part of me that was involved with those soul ties. I ask for the salvation and restoration of those people that I was involved with. I commit (him/her/them) to your care. I rebuke any evil spirits that may have gained a foothold in me from that sin. I command it to leave me now in Jesus name!
Thank you, Lord, for setting me free to live as the new person in Christ you made me to be! I praise you now and forever, Amen!"

Prayer for soul ties related to abuse.

Father God,
I release full forgiveness to those who sexually, emotionally, mentally or physically abused me. I break all soul ties related to any of these abusers. No matter how hard it is to say, bless them Lord. That they might encounter you as I have. I remove all trauma related to these soul ties. Heal these wounds that I may walk in wholeness again. I thank you for your healing and restoration to my soul.
In Jesus name Amen

Father God,
Reveal to us every tie that needs to be broken and reveal the dangers in them through these encounters. Allow us to start fresh and release us from any ungodly covenants made with others before you were leading us and we were remade. Set us free and give us the discernment to see ungodly attachments before they grow.
In Jesus Name Amen

CHAPTER 8
Be Transformed

Don't copy the behavior and customs of this world, but let God transform you into a new person by changing the way you think. Then you will learn to know God's will for you, which is good and pleasing and perfect.
Romans 12:2 NLT

If you've read this far and engaged in the prayers the release of old things that were attached from your heritage, or other ungodly connections have already been made. And you have already chosen to follow Christ, follow him closer, or reconnect with Him. Now it is time to discipline your thoughts and actions from being of this world and of the Holy Spirit instead. The ways of this world tend to portray, to each their own, success is more important than being kind, and if you are done wrong then it is okay to repay that. In the scriptures it states differently.

If we read further down in Romans 12 it states...

9 Don't just pretend to love others. Really love them. Hate what is wrong. Hold tightly to what is good. 10 Love each other with genuine affection, and take delight in honoring each other. 11 Never be lazy, but work hard and serve the Lord enthusiastically. 12 Rejoice in our confident hope. Be patient in trouble, and keep on praying. 13 When God's people are in need, be ready to help them. Always be eager to practice hospitality. 14 Bless those who persecute you. Don't curse them; pray that God will bless them. 15 Be happy with those who are happy, and weep with those who weep. 16 Live in harmony with each other. Don't be too proud to enjoy the company of ordinary people. And don't think you know it all! 17 Never pay back evil with more evil. Do things in such a way that everyone can see you are honorable. 18 Do all that you can to live in peace with everyone. 19 Dear friends, never take revenge. Leave that to the righteous anger of God. For the Scriptures say, "I will take revenge; I will pay them back," says the LORD . 20 Instead, "If your enemies are hungry, feed them. If they are thirsty, give them something to drink. In doing this, you will heap burning coals of shame on their heads." 21 Don't let evil conquer you, but conquer evil by doing good. Romans 12:9-21 NLT

So, we are called to care for even our enemies and let God handle the judgement and revenge. This is not an easy task since our flesh goes against the Spirit.

17 The sinful nature wants to do evil, which is just the opposite of what the Spirit wants. And the Spirit gives us desires that are the opposite of what the sinful nature desires. These two forces are constantly fighting each other, so you are not free to carry out your good intentions.
Galatians 5:17 NLT

19 When you follow the desires of your sinful nature, the results are very clear: sexual immorality, impurity, lustful pleasures, 20 idolatry, sorcery, hostility, quarreling, jealousy, outbursts of anger, selfish ambition, dissension, division, 21 envy, drunkenness, wild parties, and other sins like these. Let me tell you again, as I have before, that anyone living that sort of life will not inherit the Kingdom of God.
Galatians 5:19-21 NLT

Only when we walk in the Spirit by regularly communing and submitting to Him do we have the strength to walk in holiness. Our flesh is against the spirit so the one you feed will be your strongman. When we give over our lives and fill ourselves with the truth in the Word of God. We are transformed into fruitful Spirit filled beings in the likeness of Christ Jesus.

22 But the Holy Spirit produces this kind of fruit in our lives: love, joy, peace, patience, kindness, goodness, faithfulness, 23 gentleness, and self-control. There is no law against these things! 24 Those who belong to Christ Jesus have nailed the passions and desires of their sinful nature to his cross and crucified them there. 25 Since we are living by the Spirit, let us follow the Spirit's leading in every part of our lives. 26 Let us not become conceited, or provoke one another, or be jealous of one another.
Galatians 5:22-26 NLT

When things of this World tempt us to walk with it or engage in old behaviors the Word of God gives us Power to fight against the pull it has.

13 The temptations in your life are no different from what others experience. And God is faithful. He will not allow the temptation to be more than you can stand. When you are tempted, he will show you a way out so that you can endure.
1 Corinthians 10:13 NLT

Reciting the word of God especially out loud has serious power to fight Satan and the dark rulers of this world. One of the most beneficial scriptures to memorize especially when you feel attacked by our enemy.

7 Therefore submit to God. Resist the devil and he will flee from you.

James 4:7 NKJV

Another one for when struggling with the desire to even do what God wants you to, because it does happen to even the most dedicated followers.

34 Give me understanding and I will obey your instructions; I will put them into practice with all my heart. 35 Make me walk along the path of your commands, for that is where my happiness is found. 36 Give me an eagerness for your laws rather than a love for money! 37 Turn my eyes from worthless things, and give me life through your word. 38 Reassure me of your promise, made to those who fear you. 39 Help me abandon my shameful ways; for your regulations are good.
Psalm 119:34-38 NLT

In 2 Corinthians 10:3-6 it tells us how to fight this war for our soul. Our enemy is not a flesh and blood enemy. Even those in the world that seem to come against us are driven by the forces of darkness in the spirit realm.

3 For though we walk in the flesh, we are not waging war according to the flesh. 4 For the weapons of our warfare are not of the flesh but have divine power to destroy strongholds. 5 We destroy arguments and every lofty opinion raised against the knowledge of God, and take every thought captive to obey Christ, 6 being ready to punish every disobedience, when your obedience is complete.
2 Corinthians 10:3-6 NLT

    As we learn to put this first into practice, we use the authority to cast down even our sinful thoughts before they become actions and take us out. This is a powerful step into renewing our minds and transforming ourselves into the likeness of Christ. It is a process, and we will not be transformed overnight. If we seek His will and read His

Word everyday miraculous things start to happen. Getting these kinds of verses into our memory gives us the power to react quicker to the enemy's lies and shut him down. I suggest posting them on your wall, your mirror or just sitting down regularly to memorize them however you do best.

Father God,
I pray for an increased ability for those who read this to engrave your word into their hearts and give them discernment, courage, and strength to fight against our sinful natures and be transformed into who you called us to be.
In Jesus name Amen

CHAPTER 9
Enlisted

No soldier when in service gets entangled in the enterprises of [civilian] life; his aim is to satisfy and please the one who enlisted him.
2 Timothy 2:4 AMPC

Choosing to follow Christ is not all about daisies and butterflies. Yes, we get to feel the peace of Jesus through the Holy Spirit. One thing you must know as you are signing up for war, enlisted in Christ's army, choosing to fight for him or fight for the ways of this world. We are to not get entangled by the ways of this world. There is no in-between. We need to cast out any double mindedness. In James it states a double-minded man is unstable in all their ways.

6 But let him ask in faith, with no doubting, for the one who doubts is like a wave of the sea that is driven and tossed by the wind. 7 For that person must not suppose that he will receive anything from the Lord; 8 he is a double-minded man, unstable in all his ways. James 1:6-8 ESV

It is not always an easy task to stay committed to denying this world. It can get lonely physically when those around you are engaging with this world and God is telling you to withdraw. Remember again that we are not fighting against the people in the world, just the ways of this world and sin itself. Just remember if others are consumed by the world and tend to resist you, it is more than likely the Spirits in them resisting the Jesus in you not you personally. Understanding this can empower you greatly and reduce the feeling of being rejected or offended. That is why in this army, it is so important to use the weapons of our warfare given to us through Christ. They are not established through our own physical strength. They are given in prayer, meditation on the word and in the presence of Christ, and of course the power in the Word of God. We must stand firm so that we may survive.

10 Finally, be strong in the Lord and in the strength of his might. 11 Put on the whole armor of God, that you may be able to stand against the schemes of the devil. 12 For we do not wrestle against flesh and blood, but against the rulers, against the authorities, against the cosmic powers over this present darkness, against the spiritual forces of evil in the heavenly places. 13 Therefore take up the whole armor of God, that you may be able to withstand in the evil day, and having done all, to stand firm. 14 Stand therefore, having fastened on the belt of truth, and having put on the breastplate of righteousness, 15 and, as shoes for your feet, having put on the readiness given by the gospel of peace. 16 In all circumstances take up the shield of faith, with which you can extinguish all the flaming darts of the evil one; 17 and take the helmet of

salvation, and the sword of the Spirit, which is the word of God, 18 praying at all times in the Spirit, with all prayer and supplication. To that end keep alert with all perseverance, making supplication for all the saints,
Ephesians 6:10-18 ESV

Until you fully understand Spiritual Warfare and to fully utilize every piece of armor. Just begin reading this scripture OUT LOUD every morning. It can and will be a weapon of defense. We need to be BOLD and stand on the truth and the instructions God gives us.

For God has not given us a spirit of fear and timidity, but of power, love, and self-discipline.
2 Timothy 1:7 NLT

And he will not leave us!

This is my command—be strong and courageous! Do not be afraid or discouraged. For the Lord your God is with you wherever you go."
Joshua 1:9 NLT

This is not a war we fight together against mere mortals, and we are given the power through Christ himself. It is not even fought at its best by our strength or wisdom. When we seek the wisdom from the Word of God and the Holy Spirit to reveal wisdom in strategies. If we look to God for direction before making the moves, they will be the most successful and character-building ways in the end. Even when it makes no logical sense to us.

5 Trust in the LORD with all your heart, and do not lean on your own understanding. 6 In all your ways acknowledge him, and he will make straight your paths. 7 Be not wise in your own eyes; fear the LORD, and turn away

from evil. 8 It will be healing to your flesh and refreshment to your bones.
Proverbs 3:5-8 ESV

Seek Him first.
33 Seek the Kingdom of God above all else, and live righteously, and he will give you everything you need. 34 "So don't worry about tomorrow, for tomorrow will bring its own worries. Today's trouble is enough for today.
Matthew 6:33 NLT

Hold tight to His promises.
23 Let us hold tightly without wavering to the hope we affirm, for God can be trusted to keep his promise.
Hebrews 10:23 NLT

8 Rather, cling tightly to the LORD your God as you have done until now. 9 "For the LORD has driven out great and powerful nations for you, and no one has yet been able to defeat you. 10 Each one of you will put to flight a

thousand of the enemy, for the LORD your God fights for you, just as he has promised. 11 So be very careful to love the LORD your God. Joshua 23:8-11 NLT

And most of all not be afraid for the LORD will be your protection and salvation till the end and He fights for you...

14 The LORD himself will fight for you. Just stay calm."
Exodus 14:14 NLT

22 Do not be afraid of the nations there, for the LORD your God will fight for you.'
Deuteronomy 3:22 NLT

1 The LORD is my light and my salvation— so why should I be afraid? The LORD is my fortress, protecting me from danger, so why should I tremble? 2 When evil people come to devour me, when my enemies and foes attack me, they will stumble and fall. *3* Though a mighty army surrounds me, my heart will not be afraid. Even if I am attacked, I will remain confident. *4* The one thing I ask of the LORD — the thing I seek most— is to live in the house of the LORD all the days of my life, delighting in the LORD's perfections and meditating in his Temple. *5* For he will conceal me there when troubles come; he will hide me in his sanctuary. He will place me out of reach on a high rock. *6* Then I will hold my head high above my enemies who surround me. At his sanctuary I will offer sacrifices with shouts of joy, singing and praising the LORD with music. *7* Hear me as I pray, O LORD . Be merciful and answer me! *8* My heart has heard you say, "Come and talk with me." And my heart responds, " LORD, I am coming." *9* Do not turn your back on me. Do not reject your servant in anger. You have always been my helper. Don't leave me now; don't abandon me, O God of my salvation! *10* Even if my father and mother abandon me, the LORD will hold me close. *11* Teach me how to live, O LORD . Lead me along the right path, for my enemies are waiting for me. *12* Do not let me fall into their hands. For they accuse me of things I've never done; with every breath they threaten me with violence. *13* Yet I am confident I will see the LORD's goodness while I am here in the land of the living. *14* Wait patiently for the LORD . Be brave and courageous. Yes, wait patiently for the LORD. Psalms 27:1-14 NLT

Father God,
I pray for further clarity in our lives as we seek God's will and dig into your Word. It was an honor to be given this opportunity to share what the Word of God brought to my life so that more can experience the full freedom released in this one key "Jesus Christ" And the Power it brings in breaking cycles of all kinds of destruction, bondages, and even thought patterns.
Be free in the name of Jesus Amen

CHAPTER 10
Weapons to Freedom

After we commit and establish the goal to change our lives and start living for Christ. We need to start learning how to walk in the freedom and authority He gave us through our belief in Him. Can I first remind you that getting completely free isn't an overnight instant thing. For some people it can be but it will be a process. Deliverance can be more likely right now, but it may take a while to renew our minds from past thought processes. Many of us these days have many wounds and habits and thought patterns we have accumulated from this poisonous world we live in. Even though our Spirit is reborn, our soul needs some reconstruction.

Remember the soul consists of the mind, will and emotions, and those things can take some time and require dedicated persistence. By renewing your mind with the Word of God and washing your soul with it as well is an important step.

Self-discipline is also vital in changing our normal defaults. Disciplining ourselves to be in the Word every single day is one of the biggest stressors I would have to press. I also want to say that the things I share are not just my opinion but what I had to put into practice to find my own freedom. Even though I had to battle sometimes feeling like I was fully free this is what I had to do to get where I am at. The struggles are weaker and shorter lived than ever before.

When I get into perspective that I have power and authority and see the attack on me spiritually, the peace returns, and the battles subsides.

To stay in freedom, we need to stay confident that we are free, and the enemy really has already been overcome. The enemy only has power we give him. We must stand on who we are in Christ and all the power He gave us.

34 Jesus answered them, "Truly, truly, I say to you, everyone who commits sin is a slave to sin. 35 The slave does not remain in the house forever; the son remains forever. 36 So if the Son sets you free, you will be free indeed.
John 8:34-36 ESV

17 The seventy-two returned with joy, saying, "Lord, even the demons are subject to us in your name!" 18 And he said to them, "I saw Satan fall like lightning from heaven. 19

Behold, I have given you authority to tread on serpents and scorpions, and over all the power of the enemy, and nothing shall hurt you. 20 Nevertheless, do not rejoice in this, that the spirits are subject to you, but rejoice that your names are written in heaven."
Luke 10:17-20 ESV

It states here that we have authority to tread on scorpions and over ALL the power of the enemy, but he is quick to confuse us and then we give him power back.

Some of us may still require deep deliverance to increase our freedom. So, if we are struggling with things still consult God and ask the Spirit to reveal if it is a bondage of a spirit/demon or a stronghold. Consult a minister that practices deliverance or reach out to me. We deal with them in different ways. Strongholds and thoughts are pulled down or cast down.

4 For the weapons of our warfare are not carnal but mighty in God for pulling down strongholds, 5 casting down arguments and every high thing that exalts itself against the knowledge of God, bringing every thought into captivity to the obedience of Christ,
2 Corinthians 10:4-5 NKJV

And Spirits/Demons that invade us are to be cast OUT!

14 Now he was casting out a demon that was mute. When the demon had gone out, the mute man spoke, and the people marveled.
Luke 11:14 ESV

Remembering that we enlisted into an Army we need to know the weapons and armor we are entitled to along with the understanding that it is not against flesh and not even in our strength that we win the battles of life.

10 Finally, be strong in the Lord and in the strength of his might. 11 Put on the whole armor of God, that you may be able to stand against the schemes of the devil. 12 For we do not wrestle against flesh and blood, but against the rulers, against the authorities, against the cosmic powers over this present darkness, against the spiritual forces of evil in the heavenly places. 13 Therefore take up the whole armor of God, that you may be able to withstand in the evil day, and having done all, to stand firm. 14 Stand therefore, having fastened on the belt of truth, and having put on the breastplate of righteousness, 15 and, as shoes for your feet, having put on the readiness given by the gospel of peace. 16 In all circumstances take up the shield of faith, with which you can extinguish all the flaming darts of the evil one; 17 and take the helmet of salvation, and the sword of the Spirit, which is the word of God, 18 praying at all times in the Spirit, with all prayer and supplication. To

that end keep alert with all perseverance, making supplication for all the saints,
Ephesians 6:10-18 ESV

The only offensive weapon we have in our armor is the sword that is the Word of God. So, we need to know it on our tongue, to damage anything with it. Otherwise, we are just swinging around an invisible imaginary weapon.

Some more promises of our authority are...

3 And you, who were dead in your trespasses and the uncircumcision of your flesh, God made alive together with him, having forgiven us all our trespasses, 14 by canceling the record of debt that stood against us with its legal demands. This he set aside, nailing it to the cross. 15 He disarmed the rulers and authorities and put them to open shame, by triumphing over them in him.
Colossians 2:13-15 ESV

1 And he called to him his twelve disciples and gave them authority over unclean spirits, to cast them out, and to heal every disease and every affliction.
Matthew 10:1 ESV

The more we use our weapons the more skilled we become in using the correct ones and increase the strength within each attack. Staying in a continuous mindset of prayer also increased our vital connection to the source of strength which is the Holy Spirit sent by our savior Jesus Christ.

18 praying at all times in the Spirit, with all prayer and supplication. To that end keep alert with all perseverance, making supplication for all the saints,
Ephesians 6:18 ESV

This might be the final chapter in this book but remember your battle will not cease till Jesus comes back. So, continue to study your weapons by reading and meditating on the Word of God and staying close to Him in Spirit and standing in obedience. This is not only an encouragement to start and increase a walk to follow Jesus. Let this be what fans the flames so you too will spread the same encouragement and fire for the Truth!

For more detailed access to understanding the weapons and authority. I encourage you to get my "Strategies from Heaven" Spiritual battle plan workbook.

Father God,
I ask that you release discernment to ALL who read this book. Even for some to see deeper in the Spirit and help them in understanding your mysteries and your will for them. In Jesus name I claim freedom for those who have made it this far. Give them vision for what you have implanted in them and how to access it
In Jesus name Amen

FINAL THOUGHTS

We have covered many areas on establishing a relationship with Christ, rebuilding one and freeing us from our ancestral sins and past soul ties, that can keep us tied down in bondage and a cycle of turmoil seeming endless. But now what? Being a true follower of Jesus Christ not only consists of voicing our beliefs, repenting, and going to church but we are called to be and go make disciples. Disciples are students and we ourselves need first be students to show others how to successfully be disciples.

19 Go therefore and make disciples of all nations, baptizing them in the name of the Father and of the Son and of the Holy Spirit, Matthew 28:19 ESV

    I don't mean go to church and listen to only what the preacher gives you. Read the Word regularly on your own time. Ask the Holy Spirit to give you understanding of what it means and study it passionately. The things that will change in your life by disciplining yourself to learn the Word will blow your mind. Your understanding of things that used to baffle you will finally make clear sense. More than anything, get enrolled in bible studies and discipleship classes at your church. If yours does not offer them, find one that does. Or I can send you places that offer word-based training to further equip you. It will strengthen your walk and prepare you for the days ahead to stand firm for Christ.

I pray this blesses you. If you receive a breakthrough, make sure you give it to a friend and let them get freedom as well.
Also give a testimonial on how Christ encountered you to show others that freedom is possible!

Father God,
I seal all the Words of these prayers into the lives that read them and seal the freedom and deliverance of all that received it. Send strong teachers to disciple your children so they can boldly preach the Word and the power of its freedom as well. Fill them all with your Holy Spirit and let that Holy Fire burn them into purity.
In Jesus name Amen

Bible Study Materials

For further studies and teachings please visit the ministry webpage https://www.comeasyoube.com/. Get free printable studies, link to YouTube channel of teachings and prophetic words and access to download and print a full transcript of ALL my published books. No matter what your finances look like your freedom can still be accessible!! God bless this journey to walk closer with and like Christ.

In Jesus Name Amen

Made in United States
Troutdale, OR
02/28/2026